How the
Group of
20 Works

Cooperation Among the World's Major Economic Powers

Corona Brezina

Southern High Media Center
Harwood, MD 20776

ROSEN
PUBLISHING®

New York

Published in 2013 by The Rosen Publishing Group, Inc.
29 East 21st Street, New York, NY 10010

Library of Congress Cataloging-in-Publication Data

Brezina, Corona.
How the Group of 20 works: cooperation among the world's major
economic powers/Corona Brezina.—1st ed.
      p. cm.—(Real world economics)
Includes bibliographical references and index.
ISBN 978-1-4488-6788-2 (library binding)
1. Group of Twenty—Juvenile literature. 2. International economic
relations—Juvenile literature. 3. Economic policy—International
cooperation—Juvenile literature. I. Title.
HF1359.B745 2013
337.1—dc23
                                                                    2012003025

Manufactured in the United States of America

CPSIA Compliance Information: Batch #S12YA: For further information, contact Rosen Publishing,
New York, New York, at 1-800-237-9932.

Contents

4   Introduction

7   Chapter One
What Is the Group of 20?

17   Chapter Two
The G20's Mission and Mandate

29   Chapter Three
Membership in the G20

40   Chapter Four
The Organization and Inner
Workings of the G20

51   Chapter Five
Accomplishments of the
G20 Summits

64   Glossary

66   For More Information

70   For Further Reading

71   Bibliography

77   Index

INTRODUCTION

In the fall of 2008, the world was experiencing intense economic turmoil. Banks, financial institutions, and stock market prices were all negatively affected. Ordinary people began worrying about their job security and the possible disappearance of their savings. A financial crisis that had begun on Wall Street began to spread across the world, deepening into a worldwide recession.

World leaders called for a meeting in which they could discuss the crisis and adopt strategies to restore financial stability. In Washington, D.C., President George W. Bush began planning the details of the meeting, but he faced a dilemma: What nations should he invite to this crucial summit? In the past, the Group of 7 (or Group of 8, including Russia) had been the leading economic forum. It included a handful of the world's wealthiest industrialized nations. But in 2008, this forum excluded many of the world's largest developing economies.

President George W. Bush welcomes leaders from the European Union, Britain, Russia, Mexico, Indonesia, and Brazil to Washington, D.C. They had assembled for the emergency G20 summit held in November of 2008.

Instead, Bush called together a summit of the Group of 20, a forum of key industrialized and developing nations. Appropriately, the G20 had been formed in the aftermath of the Asian financial crisis of the late 1990s. It was established with the goal of promoting cooperation between industrialized and developing economies on important international economic issues. The G20 includes the wealthy G7 nations (France, Germany, Italy, Japan, the United Kingdom, the United States, and Canada), but it also included developing nations from

Asia, Africa, and South America. The other G20 members are: Argentina, Australia, Brazil, China, the European Union, India, Indonesia, Mexico, Russia, Saudi Arabia, South Africa, the Republic of Korea (South Korea), and Turkey.

On November 15, 2008, leaders of the G20 nations convened for the first time (previously, G20 meetings had only involved the nations' finance ministers). The world leaders met to "review progress being made to address the current financial crisis, advance a common understanding of its causes, and, in order to avoid a repetition, agree on a common set of principles for reform of the regulatory and institutional regimes for the world's financial sectors," as stated by a White House press release. The very act of holding the summit helped reassure the people of the world that their leaders were sincere in their promises to cooperate in restoring global economic health. The goals were ambitious—too ambitious for a hastily planned summit. Yet the G20 made some progress toward a cooperative and coordinated response to the economic and financial crisis and agreed to meet again to follow up on the work that had begun.

Since then, the group has held regular leadership summit meetings. It has expanded its scope, addressing a range of issues confronting the global economy from energy security to trade imbalances. The 2011 leadership summit held in Cannes, France, however, saw the G20 return to its roots, once again addressing a financial crisis. The debt crisis in Europe overshadowed the wide-ranging roster of more mundane topics planned for the agenda. In contrast to 2008, however, the leaders did not reach a consensus on restoring economic order. The G20 has become the leading forum for global economic cooperation, but it has not yet found a way to guarantee agreement on tough and divisive issues.

CHAPTER ONE

WHAT IS THE GROUP OF 20?

"The world is changing." Throughout history, people have made this claim when observing that things aren't the same as they used to be. In the 1990s, however, a new term arose to describe the forces changing the world: globalization. Advocates maintained that globalization brought economic opportunities to people in emerging economies. Critics claimed that it benefited wealthier nations at the expense of the poor and that any economic benefits were outweighed by the indirect costs of globalization, such as environmental degradation and exploitation of workers.

During this period of turmoil, the G20 emerged as a political and economic forum qualified to oversee sustainable economic growth in the new globalized world. It brings together a balanced membership of developed (wealthy and industrialized) and "emerging" or "developing" (often newly industrialized, but with a lower average standard of living) economies. In particular, the G20 gives a more prominent role to Asian nations than previous economic forums. By including important emerging

7

economies such as China and India, leaders of industrialized nations hoped to give them an incentive to take on more responsibility in maintaining the stability of the international financial system.

AN ECONOMICALLY INTERCONNECTED WORLD

During the 1990s, the global economy began to experience a period of dramatic change. A number of factors arose that forced world leaders to reevaluate traditional forums for addressing global economic challenges.

Emerging economies began to play a greater role on the world economic stage. Emerging economies are countries undergoing a period of economic development and reform. Although they generally experience rapid economic growth during this phase, the transition to a developed economy can bring political and social instability. Emerging economies include both major economic powers, such as China and India, and smaller economies, such as Chile and Ghana.

The 1990s also saw an increase in trade across national borders. Much of this growth was because of emerging economies opening up their markets to other countries. New free trade agreements facilitated the process. An international treaty called the General Agreement on Tariffs and Trade (GATT), which had been established in 1949, was gradually expanded. In the mid-1980s, GATT increased its scope to include developing nations in its negotiations for the first time. In 1995, GATT was replaced by the World Trade Organization (WTO), an international body that oversees international trade among its 153 member nations. During this period, many individual nations also negotiated free trade agreements, many of them regional.

A metalworker works in a steel factory in China, the world's biggest steel producer. China has emerged as a major world economy since the 1990s due to its export-driven economic growth.

The North American Free Trade Agreement (NAFTA), for example, eliminated trade barriers among the United States, Canada, and Mexico.

Investment across borders also increased. Developed and emerging economies alike liberalized their domestic capital markets. This meant that it was easier for foreigners to make investments in these economies. Investors in developed nations saw opportunities for profit in the faster-growing, emerging economies. Emerging economies increased their cross-border investments as well.

The world was entering a new era of globalization and economic integration. The reduction of barriers to trade and investment allowed emerging economies to participate

9

more fully in the global economy. But economic integration also brought greater economic interdependence. In the past, an economic downturn in a single nation would not dramatically affect the economy of the entire world. Now, such an event would also affect the nation's trading and investment partners. From there, the consequences would ripple throughout the entire global economy.

Beginning in the 1970s, a handful of developed nations, called the Group of Seven (G7) met periodically to discuss issues of global economic importance. This small group of wealthy nations dominated the agenda and decision making on behalf of the world economy. During meetings, leaders discussed the most pressing economic and political matters. They made decisions and established policy regarding these issues. The participating nations would make pledges or undertake commitments to address various economic challenges.

By the early 1990s, however, the dominance of the G7 nations in the world economy had begun to decline. Emerging economies made up a greater share of the global gross domestic product (GDP). This meant that actions taken by the G7 were no longer sufficient to steer the world economy without participation by these emerging economies.

REACTING TO CRISIS

In 1997, a financial crisis rocked a number of developing countries in Asia. Their economies were booming, but financial regulations had not kept pace with economic growth. The crisis began in Thailand. Over the next two years, it affected other countries in the region, especially South Korea and Indonesia.

Other Global Economic Forums

The Group of 20 was able to draw on the lessons and precedents set by earlier economic forums. During the mid-1970s, finance officials from the world's five largest economies—the United States, Great Britain, Italy, Japan, and West Germany—occasionally held informal meetings to discuss pressing economic matters. Collectively, they were dubbed the Group of 5 (G5). In 1975, France held an official meeting of the leaders of the six largest economies. The Group of 6 (G6) agreed to hold annual meetings. The G6 became the Group of 7 (G7) when Canada joined in 1976. In 1998, Russia was invited to join, and the Group of 8 (G8) came into existence. Finance officials of the G7 continue to hold meetings without Russian participation.

Developing economies have also established their own forums. The Group of 15, created in 1989, currently includes eighteen developing nations in Africa, Asia, South America, and Oceania. The Group of 77, formed in 1964, and the Group of 24, formed in 1971, also represent the interests of developing nations. Confusingly, in 2003, a trade bloc of developing nations dubbed itself the Group of 20. This group is not affiliated with the G20 economic forum.

These countries saw the values of their currency decline. Stock markets fell sharply. Their economies stagnated, reversing their upward trend of growth. International investors pulled money out of these troubled economies. Soon, the crisis spread beyond Asia, also affecting Russia and Latin America.

The International Monetary Fund (IMF) is an international organization representing 187 countries that is committed to maintaining financial stability, international trade, sustainable economic growth, high employment levels, and global monetary cooperation. It stepped in to provide support to stricken economies in the form of relief packages. This financial support was conditional. Governments accepting aid were required to enact financial reforms that would prevent similar crises in the future.

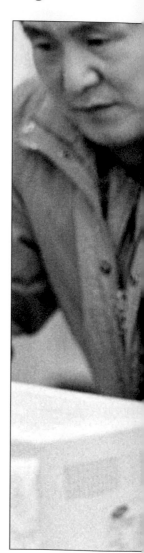

The IMF intervention only addressed the short-term economic problems in some of the affected nations. Moreover, the IMF's actions sparked controversy. Some of the conditions attached to the aid packages proved hugely unpopular. Stronger actions were needed to contain the Asian financial crisis and restore financial stability.

In April of 1998, finance ministers and central bank governors from across the world met in Washington, D.C. The participants included representatives from many of the troubled Asian economies. Since twenty-two nations took part, the assembly was dubbed the Group of 22 (G22). The meeting was organized by the U.S. Department of the Treasury, which hoped to facilitate an informal debate on the issues facing the international economy and come to an agreement on possible solutions. After the initial meeting, the group reconvened in October.

The G22 issued three reports following the conclusion of the second summit meeting. One recommended greater transparency in financial transactions. Another advised that troubled economies comply with international standards in their financial

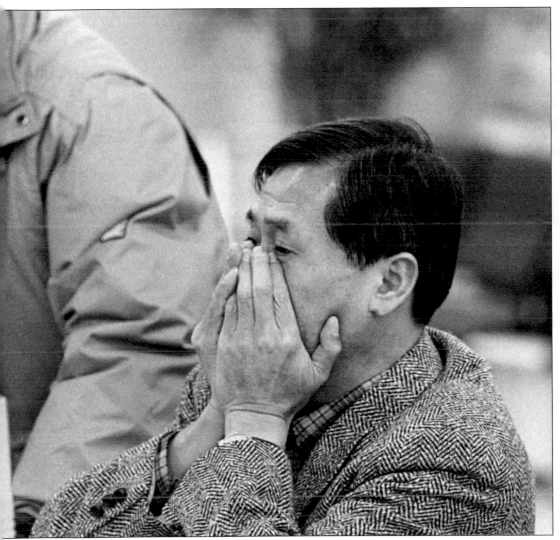

South Korean investors react to bad economic news during the financial crisis of 1997, which led to numerous corporate bankruptcies, a plunging stock market, and a steep decline in GDP.

systems. A third examined future strategies for dealing with financial crises. The reports and the outcome of the meetings were well-received internationally. They demonstrated that developed and emerging economies could cooperate effectively in addressing economic issues of global importance.

In 1999, a group representing thirty-three countries (G33) convened to follow up on the issues discussed by the G22. The members of the G7 hoped to win support for its proposals regarding international financial reforms. Emerging economies welcomed the opportunity to participate in the debate. But the G22 and G33 were both ad hoc measures. This means they were meant as onetime gatherings, designed to address a specific crisis and not meant to become a permanent global economic forum. Yet many participants, from developed and emerging economies alike, began to call for the establishment of a new and permanent forum for regular dialogue that included both developed and emerging economies.

HAMMERING OUT THE DETAILS

The members of the G7 began discussing plans for a successor to the G33 soon after the meetings concluded. In June of 1999, a G7 statement pledged its "commitment to work together to establish an informal mechanism for dialogue among systemically important countries." Paul Martin, Canada's finance minister, was one of the strongest advocates for the formation of what would become the G20.

Several practical issues had to be resolved before the new forum could come into existence. What would be the group's mandate? Some nations, such as Canada, argued that all nations would benefit if emerging economies were included in global discussions of economic matters. Others, such as France, held that a new economic forum would undermine the authority of existing institutions, such as the IMF. Initially, the proposed new forum of developing and developed nations was intended to have the narrow focus of promoting global financial stability. This was a direct reaction to the Asian crisis. As discussions went on, however, the proposed mandate for the new forum expanded.

Another key issue was the membership of the new group. What criteria would be used to select the nations invited to join? The G22 and the G33 meetings revealed that debate was more effective and successful within a smaller group. The G33 was too large and unwieldy for productive discussion. But this meant that some nations that had participated in the G22 and G33 would be cut out of the new forum.

Representatives of G20 nations pose during the inaugural 1999 meeting in Germany. Attendees include former U.S. Federal Reserve Chairman Alan Greenspan (*second from right*) and European Central Bank President Wim Duisenberg (*third from left*).

In the end, no formal conditions were set for membership. Instead, a number of factors were considered in narrowing down the selections. The members would have to be among the world's major economies (therefore, all of the G7 nations were included). The members would have to represent a diverse range of interests in the global economy. The new forum would also have to include members from each of the various regions of the world.

European membership posed a dilemma. Four European G7 members were included—Great Britain, France, Germany, and Italy. In order to maintain a small group and diverse representation, however, some European nations with large economies would be excluded in favor of smaller emerging economies. It was decided that the European Union (EU) would be included as one of the members. The EU—an economic and political partnership of twenty-seven European nations—would serve as representative for the European nations denied membership. The membership of the G20 has remained unchanged since its inception. Although there has been mild controversy over the selection of members, it has not become a point of serious contention.

In September of 1999, the G7 announced the formation of this new global economic forum. According to its formal statement, "In December in Berlin, we [the G7] will invite our counterparts from a number of systemically important countries from regions around the world to launch this new group." The first meeting of the G20 convened on December 15–16, 1999, in Germany. Hans Eichel, Germany's finance minister, hosted the meeting. Canada's Paul Martin, one of the group's key proponents, served as chairman.

CHAPTER TWO

THE G20'S MISSION AND MANDATE

The Asian financial crisis of the late 1990s was the catalyst that led to the creation of the G20. Before this, the leaders of the world's wealthy industrialized nations had begun to recognize the need for a new forum that would facilitate international economic cooperation, but most did not consider it a high priority. The Asian crisis forced the international community into action.

THE PRECEDENT OF BRETTON WOODS

This was not the first time that a crisis spurred economic reform. In 1944, the world stood at a crossroads. Representatives from forty four nations gathered in Bretton Woods, New Hampshire, to establish a new international monetary system. During the 1930s, trade barriers and currency manipulation had contributed to economic tumult. The organizers of the Bretton Woods conference hoped to negotiate a new framework that would prevent such a crisis from reoccurring. Another consideration

John Maynard Keynes (*center*), an influential economist, presented Britain's proposed monetary plan at the 1944 conference at Bretton Woods. The final plan adopted, however, was based largely on the U.S. plan.

was the economic consequences of World War II, which had not yet ended. European nations anticipated that the postwar reconstruction would be a costly effort. At Bretton Woods, they hoped to secure economic assistance from the United States.

The conference's goal, therefore, was to set up a new system that would promote international trade and revitalize the global economy. The key accomplishment was an agreement to fix the value of national currencies to gold, which was linked to the U.S. dollar. This was a monetary system known as the gold standard. By tying the value of the nations' currencies to actual gold reserves, the runaway inflation that characterized the interwar years for nations like Germany would be more easily avoided. Two organizations were created to regulate the new system: the IMF and the International Bank for Reconstruction and Development (now the chief institution of the World Bank). The Bretton Woods currency system terminated in 1971.

The ongoing influence of Bretton Woods, however, was seen in the opening lines of the statement issued after the inaugural G20 meeting: "The G20 was established to provide a new mechanism for informal dialogue in the framework of the Bretton Woods institutional system, to broaden the discussions on key economic and financial policy issues among systemically significant economies and promote co-operation to achieve stable and sustainable world economic growth that benefits all." Even though the Bretton Woods system had ended decades previously, it succeeded in setting a precedent for international economic cooperation. In particular, the Bretton Woods institutions—the IMF and the World Bank—have both grown in scope and influence since their inception. Representatives from both organizations participate in G20 meetings.

MANDATE AND PRIORITIES

During preliminary discussions at the first G20 summit, it was assumed that the IMF and the World Bank would be included in the new forum. Their precise role was a point of debate, however. In the end, it was decided that the IMF and the World Bank would attend G20 meetings as ex officio members. This meant that they would attend by virtue of their office, or their standing and influence in the world of international economics.

Participants in the first G20 meeting in Berlin, Germany, clarified the group's mandate. Early on, in the wake of the Asian financial crisis, the G20 focused on promoting financial and economic stability. The early meetings focused on matters such as creating sound national financial policies, establishing international financial standards, managing sovereign debt, maintaining consistent exchange rates, and addressing the challenges posed by globalization. An ongoing topic of debate has been reforms to the IMF and World Bank, which many developing nations view as too powerful and intrusive in nations' internal affairs and policymaking. Some of the G20's recommendations have led to changes at those institutions.

What Is a Central Bank?

Before 2008, G20 meetings were attended by finance ministers from member countries. The finance ministry is the governmental department that deals with economic and financial policy and management. In the United States, it is known as the Department of the Treasury.

In addition, G20 participants included heads of member nations' central banks. The central bank in the United States is called the Federal Reserve. A central bank is a government institution that manages a nation's money. It is responsible for controlling the supply of money and credit. The central bank regulates financial institutions and even bails them out in times of financial crisis. It also provides a variety of services, such as issuing currency and acting as the government's banker. Central banks use their considerable powers to promote full employment among the workforce and maintain stable prices. It is also the central bank's responsibility to respond to financial crises and institute reforms that will prevent their reoccurrence.

The G20's priorities have expanded to reflect whatever the most pressing challenges to the global economy are at the moment. In November 2001, for example, the group's communiqué, released after the annual meeting, expressed its collective reaction to the 9/11 terrorist attacks, including the adoption of a plan for cutting off financing to terrorist organizations. As the urgency of the Asian financial crisis waned and the world's economy absorbed the shock of the 9/11 events, the G20 broadened the scope of the issues it considered.

21

The World Economy
November 17, 2001

IMF Director Horst Kohler (*left*) and IMF Chairman Gordon Brown chat prior to a 2001 G20 finance ministers' meeting held in Ottawa, Canada.

Subsequent meetings addressed topics such as global poverty, energy conservation, the WTO negotiations, and the economic impact of aging populations, climate change, and commodity prices (commodities are basic goods such as oil, iron, wheat, and rice).

In 2008, one subject dominated the November G20 meeting in São Paulo, Brazil: the impact of the ongoing global financial crisis often referred to as the Great Recession. Little else was addressed when the G20 convened. Once again, the G20 had returned to its original mission of restoring financial stability. The top priority conveyed in the final communiqué was that the members of the G20 were committed to working together to deal with the crisis and promote a strong and lasting economic recovery.

An Evolving Organization

Until 2008, the G20 kept a low profile. Its annual meetings of finance ministers, government bureaucrats, and the heads of member nations' central banks received scant media coverage compared to the attention given to G7 and G8 conferences. Attendance was intentionally limited to facilitate informal discussion and minimize media hype and hysteria.

This practice changed after the onset of the 2008 financial crisis. Less than a month after the annual meeting, President George W. Bush convened an emergency leaders' summit of G20 members in Washington, D.C. Presidents, prime ministers, and other important officials from nations across the world met to discuss how to resolve the crisis. The summit was considered a success, and leaders' summits have continued to be held regularly. The annual meeting of finance ministers and heads of central banks occurs separately from the leadership conference.

In 2009, at the leaders' summit held in Pittsburgh, Pennsylvania, the leaders' statement issued after the conference

World leaders, including United Nations Secretary General Ban Ki-moon (*top left*), line up for a photo during the emergency Washington, D.C., G20 summit held in November of 2008.

proclaimed, "We designated the G20 to be the premier forum for our international economic cooperation." This signified that the G20 now overshadowed the G8 as the world's leading economic forum.

A More Inclusive Forum

Despite the lack of formal criteria for membership, the nations that make up the G20 represent a broad swath of the world's population and wealth. It is much more inclusive than the G7 (or G8, when Russia participates), the other major economic forum.

The member countries of the G20 represent slightly more than three quarters of the world's gross domestic product (GDP) in 2010. GDP is the value of all goods and services produced in a nation during a given time period, usually one year. Basically, it is the measure of the size of an economy. The G7, by contrast, represents only about half of the world's GDP. All of the G20 countries rank among the top thirty largest economies in the world, according to IMF data. Every nation among the world's top 25 largest economies is represented, directly or indirectly through EU membership, with two exceptions. Neither Switzerland, ranked 19th, nor Norway, ranked 24th, belong to the European Union. Representatives of both nations have expressed resentment at being excluded from G20 discussions.

A weekend crowd of Chinese shoppers flocks to Nanjing Road in Shanghai, one of the busiest shopping streets in the world. Per capita income in China has increased eightfold since the early 1980s.

The G20 also represents a greater share of the world's population. In 2010, residents of the G20 countries made up about 60 percent of the world's population. Over a third of the world's population live in China or India, which both have populations of over a billion. The G7 represented only about 11 percent of the world's population, a figure that has been steadily declining.

About 80 percent of the world's trade across borders involves G20 nations. Emerging economies have become an important force in world trade. The share of trade involving G7 nations is significantly smaller.

Geographic size is not a factor in G20 membership. However, the world's eight largest countries by land area—Russia, Canada, China, the United States, Brazil, Australia, India, and Argentina—are all members. A map of the G20 nations reveals that they cover an extensive area of the globe, especially when the European Union is included.

The European Union

The European Union was established in 1993 as a political entity made up of twelve nations. Since then, it has more than doubled its membership and formed into an economic and monetary union known as the eurozone. Seventeen EU member nations use the euro, launched in 1999, as currency. Monetary policy for the entire zone is determined by the European Central Bank. G20 meetings are attended by an EU representative, as well as a representative from the European Central Bank.

EU member states hoped that the close economic union would bolster trade and create a stable economic zone within

In 2011, Spain made deep cuts in government spending to reduce its budget deficit. Here, members of a hospital staff in Barcelona demonstrate against austerity measures.

Europe. Under a single currency, every nation would be subject to the same monetary policy. There is a huge gap between the wealthy and poorer states in the EU, however, and not all member nations have fared equally well under the euro.

The European Union was hit hard by the global financial crisis of 2008, but began making a satisfactory recovery. Then a new crisis hit. In 2009, Greece revealed that its government had amassed a huge national debt. Ireland, still recovering from the recession, was also in dire economic condition. Economists also worried about the economic health and debt load of Portugal, Italy, and Spain. The European Union and the IMF attempted to contain the debt crisis, but the EU economic situation remained unstable for a prolonged period. Much as the Asian financial crisis dominated the early G20 meetings, the EU debt crisis overshadowed the 2011 leaders' summit in Cannes, France.

THE G7

The G7 member nations played a key role in the creation of the G20. In many ways, G20 methods and procedures are based on G7 precedents. And G7 members form the G20's core of the wealthiest and most industrialized, and therefore still most influential, member nations.

Though the G7 nations are all wealthy, industrialized countries, they each face unique economic challenges. In general, industrialized nations were impacted more severely by the financial crisis and recession of 2007–2009 than emerging economies. Even within the G7, some countries, such as Canada, were less affected by the global economic downturn than others.

The United States has the world's largest economy, but the American economy has been growing at a much slower rate than that of China and some other developing nations. The United States was at the center of the global financial crisis, which dragged the economy into an eighteen-month recession, its longest downturn since the Great Depression. Once underway, the recovery progressed slowly and left many Americans dissatisfied with the sluggish state of the economy. Economic stimulus measures and decreased revenue led to large budget deficits and a swollen national debt. As a result, the United States was reluctant to involve itself financially in Europe's debt crisis or commit to any significant international economic interventions.

Japan, the world's third-largest economy, experienced spectacular economic growth from the 1960s until the late 1980s. A bursting asset bubble led to a stagnant "lost decade" during the 1990s. Although the economy improved after 2000, Japan never rebounded to its former level of economic growth. The global recession led to a reduced demand for Japan's exports. Previously, high demand for Japanese exports—especially cars and electronics—drove the nation's economic growth. In 2011, a tsunami and ensuing nuclear crisis caused calamitous damage to the country and its economy. Nonetheless, it is possible that the rebuilding effort will actually spur economic growth and possibly lift the nation out of its decades-long slump.

Germany is the world's fourth-largest economy and Europe's largest. Like Japan, it saw demands for exports fall sharply during the recession of 2007–2009. After the European debt crisis began in 2009, Germany assumed an uneasy and somewhat reluctant leadership role in the European Union. Even as Germany spearheaded actions to save the euro from collapse, many Germans balked at the prospect of bailing out economically troubled and, in their opinion, fiscally irresponsible fellow European nations. At the same time, many other Europeans resented Germany's prominent role and perceived intrusion into their domestic affairs.

France, the world's fifth-largest economy, was less affected by the global financial crisis and recession than many other developed nations. It quickly resumed healthy economic growth and, unlike some other European nations, did not hold an unmanageable load of national debt. French financial institutions, however, did hold significant Italian debt. Nonetheless, France was wary of the prospect of bailing out the troubled European economies. If the European Union agreed to write off some Italian debt, France worried that its economy would suffer the consequences.

Great Britain, the world's sixth-largest economy, was one of the few EU nations to decline adopting the euro as its currency. Since Britain's economy includes a large financial sector, the financial crisis of 2008 caused a deep and prolonged recession. As in the United States, British stimulus measures led to sharply increased budget deficits and national debt. In 2010, the government enacted an unpopular austerity program, slashing spending. The measures caused Britain's recovery to slow. Britain has chosen to remain on the sidelines of the European debt crisis, a stance that has caused some to worry about Britain's future relations with other European nations.

Italy, the world's eighth-largest economy, was severely affected by the global recession and never managed a strong recovery. Its high level of government debt, second only to Greece in Europe, threatens both Italy's economy and Europe's overall economic stability. In 2011, its economic situation

PUTTING AMERICA
TO WORK

PROJECT FUNDED
BY THE

American Recovery
and
Reinvestment Act

PEDESTRIAN
CROSSING

SLOW

MILE
5
3

In 2009, Congress enacted the American Recovery and Reinvestment Act.
This was a stimulus package intended to create jobs, such as transportation
infrastructure work, and provide relief from the impact of the Great Recession.

forced the resignation of its longtime prime minister, Silvio Berlusconi. He was replaced by an experienced economist who immediately instituted spending cuts and tax increases.

Canada, the world's tenth-largest economy, weathered the recession better than most developed nations and quickly moved into recovery. Canada's economy is closely tied to that of the United States, which is its primary market for exports.

BRICS: BRAZIL, RUSSIA, INDIA, CHINA, AND SOUTH AFRICA

In referring to the emerging economies of Brazil, Russia, India, and China, an economist coined the acronym BRIC in 2001. At this time, all four were large economics at about the same level of development. Brazil, India, and China, in particular, were experiencing dramatic economic growth. Neither India nor China experienced a recession during the global economic downturn, and Brazil quickly rebounded from a short recession. The economic growth rates of these nations declined slightly during mid-2011, however, so their long-term outlook became difficult to predict.

The four nations formed a political alliance that was later joined by South Africa, transforming "BRIC" into "BRICS." However, most economists do not consider South Africa to be an economy on the same scale as the other four.

China, the world's second-largest economy, has maintained an impressive average annual growth rate of nearly 10 percent during the last thirty years. During this time, its economy increased by about tenfold. China experienced a slowing of economic growth during the 2007–2009 global recession but did not see an economic contraction. Much of its growth is driven by exports, and China maintains a huge trade surplus with the

Chinese workers stitch clothes in a textile factory. Economic growth in China dipped during the global recession of 2007–2009 because of reduced foreign demand for exports, but it rebounded quickly.

United States. Some economists claim that China manipulates the value of its currency, keeping the yuan artificially low. This benefits China by making its exports cheaper in other countries, but it hurts American manufacturers that cannot compete with China's cheap goods. China's undervalued currency has become a point of contention in the United States. The issue has been discussed in G20 meetings, with China largely unwilling to offer much compromise on the issue.

Brazil, the world's seventh-largest economy, is the largest economy in Latin America. Its impressive economic growth rate cooled in 2011, prompting government stimulus measures to encourage spending. India, the world's ninth-largest economy, surged during the mid-2000s and attracted

Nonmember Invitees to G20 Summits

Every leaders' summit has included heads of state belonging to nonmember nations. The practice began with the initial 2008 Washington, D.C., summit, when Spain, a nonmember with one of the world's biggest economies, lobbied to attend. Spain has participated in every subsequent summit. The host country chooses the list of invitees, which are often the chairs of important international bodies. France's 2011 summit, for example, included Equatorial Guinea, which held the chair of the African Union, and the United Arab Emirates, which was chair of the Cooperation Council for the Arab States of the Gulf.

The G20 laid out formal criteria for invitees at the 2010 Seoul summit. There would be no more than five invitees, and two would be from Africa. At the same summit, the G20 also pledged to consult more with international organizations in reaching decisions on issues.

considerable foreign investment. Its economy continued to grow during the global recession, but its rate slowed during mid-2011.

Russia, the world's eleventh-largest economy, experienced a crisis of its own in 1998 as an aftershock of the Asian financial crisis. It achieved impressive growth during its recovery, but was severely affected by the 2007–2009 global financial crisis and recession. Russia's economy is highly dependent on exports of oil and other natural resources.

South Africa, the twenty-ninth-largest economy in the world and Africa's largest, is the sole African member of the G20. It is a two-tiered economy, with advanced development concentrated in a few cities coupled with a largely undeveloped and rural countryside.

Saudi Arabia, which possesses vast oil reserves, has an economy heavily dependent on its oil production. The Saudi government is currently promoting economic development and diversification.

AUSTRALIA AND MAJOR EMERGING ECONOMIES

The remaining members of the G20 are all wealthy nations with strong, growing economies. Australia, which owes its prosperity to its natural resources such as coal and iron, only

barely slipped into recession following the global financial crisis. Mexico, on the other hand, which depends heavily on exports and remittances from the United States experienced a painful recession. The rest of the G20 members experienced economic slowdowns but were not severely impacted.

The Republic of Korea (South Korea) has seen impressive growth since the 1960s and has transformed itself from a developing nation into a fully industrialized major economy. It is the most successful of the "Asian tigers," a group of nations that thrived during the 1990s only to be set back by the Asian financial crisis. It escaped any serious economic harm during the global recession of 2007–2009.

Turkey and Indonesia are both solid economies with favorable forecasts for growth. Saudi Arabia's economy is heavily dependent on revenue from oil exports. Argentina, which experienced an economic meltdown in 2001, has since rebuilt its economy and maintained steady growth.

CHAPTER FOUR

THE ORGANIZATION AND INNER WORKINGS OF THE G20

The G20 is officially described as an "informal group," according to the G20 Research Group. This informality is an advantage in some ways and a disadvantage in others. The G20 possesses some flexibility lacking in other, more formal, bureaucratic, tradition-bound, and slow-moving political and economic institutions. In 2008, for example, in response to the growing global financial crisis, the G20 quickly transformed itself into an international leaders' forum. To outsiders, however, its flexibility can be viewed as a lack of transparency and accessibility.

In addition, the G20 is often viewed as having little authority. Its recommendations often lack "teeth"—they can't be imposed upon unwilling member nations, nor can they be enforced once they are agreed upon. The G20's main purpose is to discuss policy issues, form a consensus, and make recommendations. It does not hold formal votes, and its decisions are not binding. The G20, like the G7, has no permanent secretariat or administrative department to provide structure, continuity, centralized planning, and oversight on resolutions and member nations' compliance with them.

G20 documents often claim that its diverse membership lends it exceptional legitimacy as a global representative body. It is true that the G20 is more representative of the world's various regions and national economies, both developed and developing, wealthy and less so, than is the G7. But it is still a self-appointed group. It has no procedure for admitting new members. Despite its claims of inclusiveness, over 170 nations of the world have no voice in the forum. The G20 issues official recommendations to the highly powerful and influential IMF, World Bank, and other international institutions whose decisions and policies affect not only the wealth of nations but also the daily lives of billions of ordinary people. For this reason, many consider the forum's limited membership a cause for concern.

ADMINISTRATIVE STRUCTURE, POLICIES, AND PROCEDURES

The chair of the G20 rotates among member countries. Each year, the chair is chosen from a different region, and meetings are held in the host country. The chair for the year's meetings establishes a temporary secretariat to oversee administrative details. The year's chair also wields considerable discretion over the agenda. Therefore, hosting the G20 meetings is a high-profile responsibility. A productive meeting of the world's finance ministers and treasury secretaries can boost confidence in the condition of the global economy. A successful leaders' summit can bring positive attention to the leader of the host country, both domestically and abroad.

The present chair of the G20 also works with the past year's chair and the future chair. This management arrangement is

South Korean President Lee Myung-bak arrives at the 2011 G20 summit held in Cannes, France. As the host of the 2010 summit, South Korea participated in the Troika organizing the 2011 summit.

called the Troika. At the 2011 summit, for example, the Troika consisted of South Korea (2010), France (2011), and Mexico (2012). The system is intended to provide continuity from one year to the next. Nevertheless, critics of the G20 charge that it does not succeed in this goal and that issues tend to remain unresolved because of shifting priorities from one year to the next. For this reason, some member nations have advocated the establishment of a permanent secretariat.

G20 procedures and policies have been modified as the group has evolved. It was established early on that attendance at meetings would be kept small and participants would be high-level officials in their own countries. The groundwork for meetings and summits is laid by personal representatives called

Ex-Officio Participants: The IMF and the World Bank

The International Monetary Fund and the International Bank for Reconstruction and Development (IBRD)—now part of the World Bank—were established in 1944 to promote international economic stability and encourage free trade. The IBRD was charged with providing loans and grants for postwar reconstruction and development programs. Today, the World Bank's official goal is fighting poverty.

The IMF's original mission was to oversee exchange rates and provide countries with short-term loans. It differs in function from the World Bank in that it acts as a lender to nations in crisis. The IMF also tracks the health of the international financial system and provides technical assistance on financial and economic matters, mainly to developing countries. The IMF has increased its international presence in recent years because of the global financial crisis and recession of 2007–2009 and Europe's ensuing debt crisis. Two packages of governance reform measures that had been proposed by the G20 were approved in 2008 and 2010. They were designed to make the IMF more representative and thus more legitimate.

Both organizations have been targets of intense criticism on the grounds that they are controlled primarily by wealthy developed countries. Their actions are believed by some critics to have damaging effects on the economies, environment, public health, and cultural traditions of developing countries. The IMF has also been criticized for the economic restrictions it imposes on countries receiving loans.

Sherpas. Each member nation appoints a Sherpa who is in charge of much of the behind-the-scenes negotiations. Sherpas hold advance meetings, communicate with their counterparts from other nations, and draft preliminary documents. They are

Officials representing international economic and labor organizations meet with German Chancellor Angela Merkel (*center*) during a 2011 meeting on international monetary system reform held in Germany.

experienced diplomats, often holding some sort of deputy rank in a government department.

Preparations are also supported by working groups and experts groups. The four working groups include Framework for Strong, Sustainable, and Balanced Growth; Anti-Corruption; Development; and International Monetary Fund Quota and Governance Reform. The three experts groups include Financial Inclusion, Trade Finance, and Energy. Each group is generally led by two chairpersons, one from an advanced economy and one from an emerging economy. Australia and South Africa, for example, cochaired the IMF Working Group at the 2010 Seoul summit. The groups also include experts from G20 nations, nonmember nations, and international organizations. Participants analyze relevant issues, discuss proposed actions, and prepare reports.

The G20 cooperates with international organizations in meetings and preparation. The IMF and World Bank are official participants, but the G20 also invites input from other relevant groups, such as the Organization for Economic Co-operation and Development (OECD), the WTO, and the United Nations (UN). Experts from these groups, as well as private entities and nongovernmental organizations (NGOs), may participate in meetings on their topics of expertise. (NGOs are generally nonprofit groups with an interest in a specific cause, such as the environment or human rights.)

MINISTERIAL MEETINGS

G20 ministerial meetings, held annually in the autumn, usually take place over two or three days. The host country plans the events and sets the schedule for the participants. The proceedings are not open to the press or public. The results of the meeting are publicized shortly after the meeting is concluded in the form of a communiqué. Individual working groups may also release papers on their subject. Individual G20 members may also issue statements on the outcome of the meeting, though this is more common following the higher-profile leaders' summits. After the ministerial meeting, various official groups release reports such as analyses, commentaries, and compliance reports.

The G20's main mission is to provide a forum for discussion and attempts to reach a consensus on issues. Over time, the G20 has expanded its mandate by considering new issues, while other issues have fallen off its agenda without being resolved. At four of its meetings between 1999 and 2004, for example, the G20 addressed the issue of capital account liberalization. Members called for a relaxing of restrictions on moving capital between countries. The issue ceased to be brought up after 2004.

In 2000, at a meeting in Montreal, Canada, participants first addressed the issue of globalization. The G20 affirmed its commitment to global economic integration and made suggestions on how to support emerging economies dealing with the effects of globalization. It also expanded its list of recommendations on how nations could reduce their vulnerability to financial crisis.

The 2001 meeting, held in Ottawa, Canada, took place shortly after the 9/11 terrorist attacks. Combating terrorist financing became a new priority. The G20 joined a number of other international organizations committed to cooperating in the effort.

Central bankers and finance ministers convene for the 2004 G20 meeting held in Berlin, Germany, which focused on promoting international financial stability and sustainable economic growth.

At the 2002 meeting, held in New Delhi, India, the G20 addressed the issue of development and aid to developing nations. In particular, it praised the growing international support for sustainable development in Africa. The 2003 meeting

Australian Treasurer Peter Costello formally opens the 2006 G20 meeting held in Melbourne. One outcome of the meeting was agreement on historic reforms to the IMF.

in Morelia, Mexico, continued to examine some of the G20's key issues, including globalization, financial reform, terrorist financing, and development. There, the G20 took up for the first time the topic of global fiscal imbalances. The heart of this issue is how some countries tend to save or invest money prudently, fostering sustained growth and development, while others run up massive and destabilizing debts that can often result in economic crisis and collapse.

In 2004, Berlin, Germany, hosted the annual G20 meeting. Following the meeting, the G20 issued two documents that presented the results of much of its work on strengthening the financial system. The *G20 Accord for Sustained Growth* presented the key tasks that governments had to address in order to promote long-lasting growth. The *G20 Reform Agenda* outlined policy measures that would achieve the points presented in the *Accord*. To demonstrate their commitment to the process, member nations each described concrete policy actions they intended to take. Participants also took up the issue of energy policy for the first time, emphasizing the importance of energy efficiency and alternative energy sources.

The 2005 meeting, hosted in Xianghe, China, featured a new focus on development issues, rather than the financial reform emphasis of previous years. For the

NORS

Zhou

Jin

49

first time, the forum discussed possible reforms to the Bretton Woods institutions—the IMF and the World Bank. The G20 indicated that developing nations merited a greater voice in these institutions, especially since the World Bank and IMF exerted so much influence over these governments' domestic and economic policies. It stated that the IMF should take "changes in economic weight" of thriving emerging economies into consideration when dictating policy. It also recommended more effective cooperation between the World Bank and IMF and improvements in their operations and management. In subsequent meetings, the issue of reforming these institutions continued to be a major priority for the G20.

Australia, which hosted the 2006 meeting in Melbourne, viewed its chairmanship as an opportunity to emphasize the G20's mandate to steer the world economy effectively and judiciously. Energy and minerals security was also a high-priority issue for the Australians. In addition, the G20 continued to address its core issues during the Melbourne conference, focusing in particular on reforms to the IMF and World Bank. The G20 praised the two institutions for acknowledging the need for reform, reiterated its 2005 position, and vowed that the G20 would continue to address "strategic and policy issues" involving the two institutions at future meetings.

The 2007 meeting, held in Kleinmond, South Africa, adopted "Sharing—Influence, Responsibility, and Knowledge" as its theme. Participants continued building on the successes of the Melbourne meeting. Because the world economy was experiencing turbulence that eventually led to the financial crisis and a global recession, the topic of "Global Outlook" took priority in the final communiqué.

CHAPTER FIVE

ACCOMPLISHMENTS OF THE G20 SUMMITS

In September 2008, a troubled American economy reached the point of financial meltdown. Big banks and financial institutions threatened to fail. The U.S. government took over management of some financial institutions and bailed out others. A major investment bank, Lehman Brothers, collapsed, stunning the financial world. The stock market fluctuated wildly, mostly plummeting downward. Around the world, other countries also saw their banks struggling and their markets in turmoil.

This chaotic scenario provided the backdrop of the November 9, 2008, G20 ministerial meeting in São Paulo, Brazil. The topic of the financial crisis dominated the meeting, but few concrete action plans emerged. Another assembly had already been scheduled for that purpose: the first G20 leaders' summit, scheduled for November 15.

Although leaders' summits now receive more attention, regular G20 ministerial meetings have continued to take place. The 2009 meeting was held in Horsham, United Kingdom;

An employee at Bear Stearns moves out of his office following the investment giant's collapse in 2008. The failed bank was taken over by JPMorgan Chase in a deal supported by the Federal Reserve.

the 2010 in Busan, South Korea; the 2011 in Paris, France. Since the onset of the global financial crisis and recession and the establishment of leaders' summits, the ministerial meetings have focused narrowly on financial stability and reforms, as well as on implementing decisions made at the leaders' summits.

CONVENING TO COMBAT THE GLOBAL FINANCIAL CRISIS

As the world was reeling from the financial crisis, some European leaders began calling for a Bretton Woods II. They had in mind a conference that would establish an updated international framework for the financial system. Some countries hoped for a bigger role for the IMF, better monitoring of financial systems, and safeguards for preventing future crises. French and British leaders, among others, called for a global summit to discuss financial reforms. President George W. Bush formally invited the leaders of the G20 to a November summit in Washington, D.C.

Even before the summit convened, however, leaders began to rein in high expectations for the meeting. The conference was assembled hastily, with events developing and changing rapidly in the background. Nevertheless, it was the most significant gathering of world leaders in nearly a decade and the first leaders' summit of the newly powerful G20. The very fact that a summit meeting had been called for and convened sent a reassuring message to the world that the leaders were serious about confronting and solving the crisis.

The leaders confirmed their commitment to working together and agreed on some basic necessary solutions, such as improving regulations and putting stimulus measures into place. The summit yielded an action plan that made recommendations in seven areas. These were: transparency and accountability, sound regulation, prudential oversight, risk management, integrity in financial markets, international cooperation, and international financial institutions. Member nations' finance ministers were charged with developing and implementing specific points for each category.

Nonetheless, the leaders made few concrete decisions or commitments. Critics pointed out that in portraying a unified front, they avoided addressing many contentious issues. Agreement on the need to strengthen regulations, for example, does not signify that there is agreement on how to do so. Leaders announced that they would hold another summit in the near future during which they would discuss the progress that had been made toward achieving the objectives of the November 2008 action plan.

Leaders' Summits

The next leaders' summit took place in London, England, on April 1–2, 2009. It served as a follow-up meeting to review the progress made since the Washington, D.C., summit of November 2008. To emphasize their commitment to taking decisive action toward addressing the worldwide financial crisis, the leaders titled their final statement "Global Plan for Recovery and Reform." The document listed a number of general goals, such as restoring growth and jobs, strengthening financial regulations, and funding and reforming international financial institutions. Leaders also backed up their words with financial commitments, especially in pledges to enact stimulus measures and bolster the IMF.

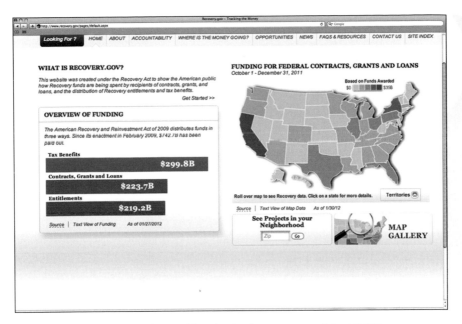

Some critics were alarmed by the high price tag of the 2009 American Recovery and Reinvestment Act. The Web site Recovery.gov aimed to demonstrate that the funds were being put to good use.

The G20 held another leaders' summit six months later in Pittsburgh, Pennsylvania. In their concluding statement, leaders described the economy as being in a "critical transition from crisis to recovery." The G20 lauded international cooperation and identified some successes in addressing the economic crisis, such as effective stimulus measures. Leaders agreed to participate in a new "Framework for Strong, Sustainable, and Balanced Growth," in which nations would set objectives and institute policies that would help achieve them. The IMF and the World Bank would assist in overseeing the implementation of the Framework objectives. The G20 also put forth proposals for significant reforms to the IMF that included granting a greater voting share to developing nations. These were formally approved in 2010. In addition to issues concerning financial stability and reform, the G20 touched on issues such as energy security and climate change.

In 2010, as Europe was beginning to struggle with its debt crisis, the Canadian city of Toronto hosted the next leaders' summit. Leaders arriving at the summit held divergent views on how to approach both the debt crisis and the continued sluggish economic recovery following the end of the Great Recession. Germany, for example, supported a policy of reduced government spending to reduce budget deficits. The United States held that continued stimulus measures would help prevent another economic downturn. In a compromise, the G20 set a goal of cutting budget deficits in half by 2013. The G20 continued to discuss financial reforms and the promotion of trade, but members failed to agree on concrete measures, such as enacting a global bank tax or implementing new rules for banks.

Later in 2010, South Korea became the first non-G8 member to host a leaders' summit. The theme for the event was "Shared Growth Beyond Crisis." Despite the cooperative tone struck by this theme, many observers noted that member

G20 participants at the 2011 Cannes summit failed to come to an agreement on the issue of China's currency valuation. Some economists believe China's currency, the yuan, is held artificially low to promote Chinese exports.

nations had lost the sense of urgency that had promoted compromise and coordinated action in earlier summits. In Seoul, participants were more committed to their national economic self-interests than the global good.

Protesting the G20

Ever since the 2009 G20 summit in London, England, the meetings have attracted substantial protests. Demonstrators focus their protests on the negative effects of economic policies, corporate influence, globalization, and a wide variety of other issues ranging from climate change to poverty. Thousands of protesters typically converge on the summit site.

On some occasions, the demonstrations became high-profile and controversial events in their own right. At the 2009 London summit, mostly peaceful protests turned violent in a few instances as demonstrators clashed with police. In Pittsburgh, Pennsylvania, during the autumn 2009 summit, police dispersed protestors with tear gas and a sonic cannon, a weapon never before used against U.S. citizens. At the 2010 summit in Toronto, Canada, the Canadian government instituted the toughest security measures of any previous G20 summit. In some places, protests escalated into rioting and vandalism. Nearly one thousand people were arrested by police, making it the biggest mass arrest in Canadian history.

One of the high-profile sources of disagreement of the South Korea summit was the tension between the United States and China over China's valuation of its currency. The issue was not resolved. There was also more friction over issues related to free trade and protectionism than in previous years. Participants discussed account imbalances—the issue of some nations running significant trade deficits while others maintain surpluses. Instead of reaching a consensus, however, leaders called on finance ministers and the IMF to draw up guidelines. Overall, the G20 tackled a far-reaching agenda that led to a long list of shared objectives but few concrete breakthroughs or resolutions.

THE 2011 CANNES SUMMIT

On November 2, 2011, world leaders convened in Cannes, France, for the G20 summit. The host, French president Nicolas Sarkozy, had set an ambitious agenda. A top priority was the development of an action plan that would address global imbalances in government budgets. He also called for further reforms to the IMF. Other points for discussion included sustainable development, global governance, financial regulation, agriculture, energy, climate, fighting corruption, and the social dimension of globalization, a new topic for G20 consideration.

Sarkozy's agenda was derailed, however, by dramatic developments in the ongoing European debt crisis. A negotiated bailout of debt-strapped Greece was threatened when the Greek president unexpectedly decided to put the issue before voters. Meanwhile, Italy's government had fallen into a state of political and economic turmoil that would ultimately lead to the resignation of the prime minister. The two-day summit was dominated by fallout from the developing events in Greece and the uncertain economic situation across Europe. Greece's plight raised the possibility that it could drop the euro as its currency, which would negatively impact the entire eurozone.

By the end of the summit, some of the worries over Greece had been allayed. Greece agreed to accept the bailout plan without putting it to a vote. The Greek prime minister resigned. Italy agreed to accept IMF monitoring, but its weak economy remained a cause for concern. The final communiqué of the summit offered broad promises for future actions, rather than specific commitments. Since much of the work on specific issues had been prepared ahead of the summit, the communiqué included statements pertaining to Sarkozy's long list of issues, even though most of them had not actually been discussed by the G20 leaders. The G20 also announced that Mexico would take the chair next and that the 2012 summit would be held in June in Los Cabos.

CRITICISMS OF THE G20

Ever since the G20 evolved into an influential economic forum, some critics have questioned its role in steering the global economy. There were issues raised concerning the G20's legitimacy, even in its early stages. The G20 aims to guide the global economy, yet most of the countries of the world have no representation in the body. The G20 was not approved by any international treaties. And although it is true that the G20 represents a large proportion of the world's wealth and population, the governments of most of the world's nations were never given a voice in its mandate or functioning. There have been claims that the high profile of the G20 undermines the legitimacy of more inclusive and representative international organizations such as the United

Greek protestors assemble in front of the Parliament building. European participants at the 2011 Cannes summit took the opportunity to lobby for aid from the IMF, but the G20 failed to reach a consensus on the issue.

Nations or the World Trade Organization, which does have a broad international membership.

At the same time, the G20's informal nature threatens to weaken its effectiveness. Since it operates through consensus, rather than a majority vote, a few dissenters can derail the adoption of a measure that otherwise enjoys broad and general support. The process of compromising in order to gain broad approval can reduce ambitious goals to minor policy adjustments. In addition, declarations by the G20 are not binding—the group essentially depends on peer pressure for compliance. Once commitments are made, there is generally no binding means of enforcement. Studies of compliance by the G20 Research Group find that member nations often fail to keep the promises made at summits.

Observers have noted that consensus among participants at the leaders' summits has waned since the earliest summits. Nations have tended to agree on fewer significant pledges and commitments. During the global financial crisis and recession of 2007–2009, every G20 member had a stake in restoring international economic health. Now that members are facing their own specific economic challenges and are recovering from recession at varying rates, setting a common course is more problematic. There is no guarantee that this trend will continue, however. It is possible that the G20 members will find a new resolve to cooperate on pressing issues, especially in the face of whatever turns out to be the next great global crisis.

1. What did the G20 identify as the most pressing global economic issues at the most recent summit and ministerial meetings?

2. How did the most recent meetings rate the health of the global economy?

3. Were there any significant breakthroughs on contentious issues, such as trade imbalances or currency valuations, at the most recent summit?

4. Were there any further proposed reforms of the IMF at the most recent meetings?

5. Did the most recent meetings recommend any reforms to the G20's own structure or functions?

6. How will decisions made at the most recent meetings affect U.S. economic policy?

7. When and where will the next G20 leaders' summit and the next G20 ministerial meeting be held?

8. Will there be any critical new issues up for discussion at the next meetings?

9. What are the priorities of the United States going into the next meetings?

10. How well is the G20 fulfilling its responsibilities in steering the international economy prudently and wisely? Is it operating for the good of the many or the continued enrichment of the few?

GLOSSARY

central bank An institution or agency, either associated with the government or independent, that is responsible for exercising control of a nation's monetary and financial systems.

commodity Any bulk good, especially goods that are largely unprocessed, that can be sold and traded.

compliance The act of conforming to a law, recommendation, or official requirement.

currency Something that is used as a medium of exchange; money.

debt Something that is owed or that one is bound to pay to another person or institution.

deficit The amount by which a sum of money falls short of the needed amount; the difference between the amount of money that has been spent versus the smaller amount that has been earned and collected.

export A good or service produced domestically and shipped to and sold in foreign markets.

gross domestic product (GDP) The monetary value of all of the goods and services produced in a nation during a period of time, usually a year.

industrialization The large-scale development of mechanized industry in a country.

investment Money committed in order to earn a future financial return.

mandate The authority granted to a government or official body to follow a course of action on certain issues.

monetary policy Actions taken by a central bank to change the money supply (increase it or decrease it) in order to influence economic activity.

protectionism The government policy of imposing trade barriers, such as tariffs and quotas, to protect domestic producers from foreign competition.

recession An economic downturn, usually defined as six months or more of declining GDP.

recovery The upward phase of the business cycle in which economic conditions improve and the economy resumes growth.

stimulus In economics, government-initiated measures intended to spur growth.

summit A meeting or conference of government leaders or other high-level officials.

transparency The extent to which relevant information is made public by an organization.

FOR MORE INFORMATION

Bank of Canada
234 Wellington Street
Ottawa, ON K1A 0G9
Canada
(800) 303-1282
Web site: http://www.bankofcanada.ca
The Bank of Canada is Canada's central bank.

Board of Governors of the Federal Reserve System
20th Street and Constitution Avenue NW
Washington, DC 20551
Web site: http://www.federalreserve.gov
The Federal Reserve is the central bank of the United States.

Council on Foreign Relations (CFR)
The Harold Pratt House
58 East 68th Street
New York, NY 10065
(212) 434-9400
Web site: http://www.cfr.org
The CFR is an independent, nonpartisan membership
    organization, think tank, and publisher. It is dedicated to
    being a resource for its members, government officials,
    business executives, journalists, educators and students,

civic and religious leaders, and other interested citizens in order to help them better understand the world and the foreign policy choices facing the United States and other countries. Founded in 1921, the CFR takes no institutional positions on matters of policy.

G20 Research Group
Munk Centre for International Studies
Trinity College
University of Toronto
1 Devonshire Place
Toronto, ON M5S 3K7
Canada
Web site: http://www.g20.utoronto.ca
The G20 Research Group's mission is to serve as the world's leading independent source of information, analysis, and research on the G20.

International Monetary Fund (IMF)
700 19th Street NW
Washington, DC 20431
(202) 623-7000
Web site: http://www.imf.org
The IMF is an organization of 187 countries, working to foster global monetary cooperation, secure financial stability, facilitate international trade, promote high employment and sustainable economic growth, and reduce poverty around the world.

United Nations (UN)
Public Inquiries, Visitors Services

Department of Public Information
United Nations Headquarters, Room GA-1B-57
New York, NY 10017
(212) 963-4475
Web site: http://www.un.org
The UN is an international organization committed to
    maintaining international peace, developing friendly
    relations among nations, and promoting human welfare.

U.S. Department of the Treasury
1500 Pennsylvania Avenue NW
Washington, DC 20220
(202) 622-2000
Web site: http://www.treas.gov
The U.S. Department of the Treasury's mission is to maintain
    a strong economy and create economic and job
    opportunities by promoting the conditions that enable
    economic growth and stability at home and abroad,
    strengthen national security by combating threats and
    protecting the integrity of the financial system, and
    manage the U.S. government's finances and resources
    effectively.

World Bank
1818 H Street NW
Washington, DC 20433
(202) 473-1000
Web site: http://www.worldbank.org
The World Bank provides financial and technical assistance to
    developing nations around the world.

World Trade Organization (WTO)
Centre William Rappard
Rue de Lausanne 154
CH-1211 Geneva 21
Switzerland
Tel.: +41 (0)22 739 51 11
Web site: http://www.wto.org
The WTO is the global international organization that deals
   with the rules of trade between nations.

WEB SITES

Due to the changing nature of Internet links, Rosen Publishing
has developed an online list of Web sites related to the subject
of this book. This site is updated regularly. Please use this link
to access the list:

http://www.rosenlinks.com/rwe/grp20

FOR FURTHER READING

Acton, Johnny, and David Goldblatt. *Economy*. New York, NY: DK, 2010.

Berlatsky, Noah, ed. *The Global Financial Crisis* (Global Viewpoints). San Diego, CA: Greenhaven Press, 2010.

Clifford, Tim. *Our Economy in Action*. Vero Beach, FL: Rourke Publishing, 2009.

Craats, Rennay. *Economy: USA Past Present Future*. New York, NY: Weigl Publishers, 2009.

Gorman, Tom. *The Complete Idiot's Guide to the Great Recession*. New York, NY: Penguin Group, 2010.

Hall, Alvin. *Show Me the Money: How to Make Cents of Economics*. New York, NY: DK, 2008.

Hynson, Colin. *The Credit Crunch* (The World Today). North Mankato, MN: Sea to Sea Publications, 2010.

Merino, Noel. *The World Economy* (Current Controversies). San Diego, CA: Greenhaven Press, 2010.

Miller Debra A. *The U.S. Economy* (Current Controversies). San Diego, CA: Greenhaven Press, 2010.

Steger, Manfred. *Globalization: A Very Short Introduction*. New York, NY: Oxford University Press, 2009.

Thomas, Lloyd B. *The Financial Crisis and Federal Reserve Policy*. New York, NY: Palgrave Macmillan, 2011.

Young, Mitchell, ed. *Free Trade* (Opposing Viewpoints). San Diego, CA: Greenhaven Press, 2008.

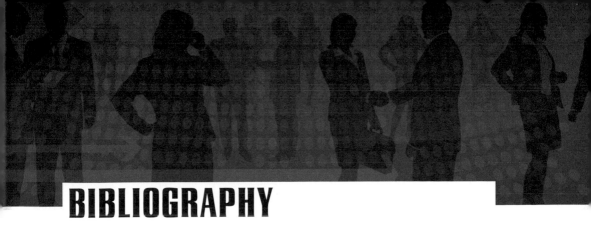

BIBLIOGRAPHY

Axilrod, Stephen H. *Inside the Fed: Monetary Policy and Its Management, Martin Through Greenspan to Bernanke.* Cambridge, MA: MIT Press, 2009.

Berensmann, Kathrin, Thomas Fues, and Ulrich Volz. "Informal Power Centre." D&C, January 2011. Retrieved December 2011 (http://www.dandc.eu/articles/184899/index.en.shtml).

Board of Governors of the Federal Reserve System. *The Federal Reserve System: Purposes and Functions.* 9th ed. Washington, DC: Board of Governors of the Federal Reserve System, 2005.

Boudreaux, Donald J. *Globalization.* Westport, CT: Greenwood Press, 2008.

Carin, Barry. "The Future of the G20 Process." Centre for International Governance Innovation, November 4, 2010. Retrieved December 2011 (http://www.cigionline.org/publications/2010/11/future-g20-process).

CNN. "Officials: G-20 to Supplant G-8 as International Economic Council." September 24, 2009. Retrieved December 2011 (http://articles.cnn.com/2009-09-24/us/us.g.twenty.summit_1_summit-crisis-fades-financial-crisis?_s=PM:US).

Davis, Bob, and Damien Paletta. "U.S. Gets Rebuffed at Divided Summit." *Wall Street Journal*, November 13,

2010. Retrieved December 2011 (http://online.wsj.com/article/SB200014240527487048657045756107616472 91510.htm).

Epping, Randy Charles. *The 21st Century Economy: A Beginner's Guide*. New York, NY: Vintage Books, 2009.

Ertel, Manfred. "Norway Takes Aim at G-20." *Spiegel Online*, June 22, 2010. Retrieved December 2011 (http://www.spiegel.de/international/europe/0,1518,702104,00.html).

Federal Reserve Bank of San Francisco. *The Federal Reserve System in Brief*. San Francisco, CA: Federal Reserve Bank of San Francisco, 2006.

Federal Reserve Bank of San Francisco. *U.S. Monetary Policy: An Introduction*. San Francisco, CA: Federal Reserve Bank of San Francisco, 2004.

G8 Research Group. "G7 Statement." G8 Information Centre, June 18, 1999. Retrieved December 2011 (http://www.g7.utoronto.ca/summit/1999koln/g7statement_june18.htm).

G8 Research Group. "Statement of G7 Finance Ministers and Central Bank Governors." G8 Information Centre, September 25, 1999. Retrieved December 2011 (http://www.g8.utoronto.ca/finance/fm992509state.htm).

Gordon, John Steele. *An Empire of Wealth: The Epic History of American Economic Power*. New York, NY: HarperCollins, 2004.

Gorman, Tom. *The Complete Idiot's Guide to the Great Recession*. New York, NY: Penguin Group, 2010.

G20 Information Centre. "The Group of Twenty: A History." 2008. Retrieved December 2011 (http://www.g20.utoronto.ca/docs/g20history.pdf).

G20 Research Group. "Communiqué." G20 Information Centre, December 1999. Retrieved December 2011 (http://www .g8.utoronto.ca/g20/1999/1999communique.htm).

G20 Research Group. "Communiqué." G20 Information Centre, November 19, 2005. Retrieved December 2011 (http://www.g20.utoronto.ca/2006/ 2006communique.html).

G20 Research Group. "G20 Analysis." G20 Information Centre. Retrieved December 2011 (http://www .g8.utoronto.ca/g20/analysis/index.html#commentary).

G20 Research Group. "G20 Leaders Statement: The Pittsburgh Summit." G20 Information Centre, September 2009. Retrieved December 2011 (http:// www.g20.utoronto.ca/2009/2009communique0925.html).

G20 Research Group. "G20 Statement on Reforming the Bretton Woods Institutions." G20 Information Centre, October 2005. Retrieved December 2011 (http://www .g20.utoronto.ca/2005/2005bwi.html).

G20 Research Group. "Statement by Press Secretary Dana Perino." G20 Information Centre, October 22, 2008. Retrieved December 2011 (http://www.g8.utoronto.ca/ g20/2008/2008announcement.html).

Hawke, Gary. "G20 Consensus, Compliance and the Limits of Legitimacy." East Asia Forum, October 26, 2010. Retrieved December 2011 (http://www.eastasiaforum .org/2010/10/26/g20 consensus compliance and the limits-of-legitimacy).

IMF. "Factsheet: A Guide to Committees, Groups, and Clubs." August 31, 2011. Retrieved December 2011 (http://www.imf.org/external/np/exr/facts/groups.htm).

IMF. "G-20 Surveillance Notes." Retrieved December 28, 2011. Retrieved December 2011 (http://www.imf.org/external/ns/cs.aspx?id=249).

IMF. "World Economic Outlook: Tensions from the Two-Speed Recovery: Unemployment, Commodities, and Capital Flow." April 2011. Retrieved December 2011 (http://www.imf.org/external/pubs/ft/weo/2011/01).

Kilpatrick, Sean. "Who Gets to Rule the World." *Maclean's*, July 1, 2010. Retrieved December 2011 (http://www2.macleans.ca/2010/07/01/who-gets-to-rule-the-world).

Landler, Mark. "World Leaders Vow Joint Push to Aid Economy." *New York Times*, November 16, 2008. Retrieved December 2011 (http://www.nytimes.com/2008/11/16/business/worldbusiness/16summit.html?pagewanted=all).

Leuthard, Doris. "We Cannot and Do Not Wish to Cede This Responsibility to a Group of Twenty Selected States." *Current Concerns*, February 2010. Retrieved December 2011 (http://www.currentconcerns.ch/index.php?id=972).

Mahoney, Jill, and Ann Hui. "G20-Related Mass Arrests Unique in Canadian History." *Globe and Mail*, June 28, 2010. Retrieved December 2011 (http://www.theglobeandmail.com/news/world/g8-g20/news/g20-related-mass-arrests-unique-in-canadian-history/article1621198).

Menon, Vanu Gopala. "Global Governance: The G-20 and the UN." TerraViva, March 29, 2010. Retrieved December 2011 (http://www.ipsterraviva.net/UN/print.aspx?idnews=N7370).

New York Times. "Group of 20." November 4, 2011. Retrieved December 2011 (http://topics.nytimes.com/top/reference/timestopics/organizations/g/group_of_20/index.html).

Prasad, Eswar. "Crisis Kills G-20 Progress." *Daily Beast*,
    November 5, 2011. Retrieved December 2011 (http://
    www.thedailybeast.com/articles/2011/11/04/g-20-
    summit-promise-of-progress-killed-by-world-financial-
    crisis.html).

Prasad, Eswar. "G-20 Is at Its Best When the Stakes Are
    Highest." *New York Times*, November 2, 2011. Retrieved
    December 2011 (http://www.nytimes.com/2011/11/03/
    business/global/g-20-is-at-its-best-when-the-stakes-
    are-highest.html).

Rieffel, Lex. "The G-20 Summit: What's It All About?"
    Brookings, October 27, 2008. Retrieved December 2011
    (http://www.brookings.edu/opinions/2008/1027_
    governance_rieffel.aspx).

Robinson, Dan. "G20 Commits to Deficit Reduction Time Line."
    VOANews, June 27, 2010. Retrieved December 2011 (http://
    www.voanews.com/english/news/americas/World-Leaders-
    Gather-for-G20-Economic-Summit-97257039.html).

Rooney, Ben. "G20 Agree to 'Action Plan' for Global
    Economy." CNNMoney, November 4, 2011. Retrieved
    December 2011 (http://money.cnn.com/2011/11/04/
    news/international/g20_summit/index.htm).

Schneider, Howard, and Scott Wilson. "President Obama Urges
    G-20 Nations to Spend; They Pledge to Halve Deficits."
    Washington Post, June 28, 2010. Retrieved December 2011
    (http://www.washingtonpost.com/wp-dyn/content/
    article/2010/06/27/AR2010062701754.html).

Thirlwell, Mark, and Malcolm Cook. "Geeing Up for the
    G-20." Lowy Institute for International Policy, April
    2006. Retrieved December 2011 (http://www.
    lowyinstitute.org/Publication.asp?pid=719).

Townsend, Ian. "G20 & the November 2010 Seoul Summit."
    Parliament.UK, October 19, 2010. Retrieved December
    2011 (http://www.parliament.uk/briefing-papers/SN05028).
Tucker, Irvin. *Economics for Today*. 3rd ed. Mason, OH:
    Thomson/South-Western, 2003.
Weaver, Matthew. "G20 Protesters Blasted by Sonic Cannon."
    Guardian, September 25, 2009. Retrieved December
    2011 (http://www.guardian.co.uk/world/blog/2009/
    sep/25/sonic-cannon-g20-pittsburgh).
Wessel, David. *In Fed We Trust: Ben Bernanke's War on the
    Great Panic*. New York, NY: Crown Business, 2009.
Wilson, Scott. "Obama at G-20 Summit Acknowledges 'Hard
    Work Ahead' on Economy." *Washington Post*, November
    4, 2011. Retrieved December 2011 (http://www
    .washingtonpost.com/politics/obama-at-g-20-summt-
    acknowledges-hard-work-ahead-on-economy/2011/
    11/04/gIQAHG75lM_story.html).
Wintour, Patrick, and Andrew Clark. "G20 Leaders Map Out
    New Economic Order at Pittsburgh Summit." *Guardian*,
    September 25, 2009. Retrieved December 2011 (http://
    www.guardian.co.uk/world/2009/sep/25/
    g20-summit-economy-bonuses-deficits).
Wintour, Patrick, and Larry Elliott. "Global Recession Grows
    Closer as G20 Summit Fails." *Guardian*, November 4, 2011.
    Retrieved December 2011 (http://www.guardian.co.uk/
    business/2011/nov/04/global-recession-g20-summit).
Wroughton, Lesley. "G20 Fails to Endorse Financial
    Transaction Rax." Reuters, November 4, 2011. Retrieved
    December 2011 (http://www.reuters.com/article/2011/
    11/04/g20-tax-idUSN1E7A302520111104).

INDEX

A

Argentina, 6, 27, 39
Asian financial crisis, 5, 10–12,
        15, 17, 20, 21, 31, 37, 39
Australia, 6, 27, 39, 45, 50

B

Berlusconi, Silvio, 33–35
Brazil, 6, 23, 27, 35, 36, 51
Bretton Woods, 17–20, 50
BRICS, 35–38
Bush, George W., 4, 23, 53

C

Canada, 5, 9, 11, 14, 16, 27, 31,
        35, 47, 56, 58
Cannes summit (2011), 6, 31,
        59–60
central banks, 21
Chile, 8
China, 6, 8, 27, 32, 35–36,
        49, 58
climate change, 22, 29, 56,
        58, 59

E

economic forums, overview of
        other, 11, 12–16, 25
Eichel, Hans, 16
euro, 30–31, 33, 59
European Central Bank, 30
European Union, 6, 16, 25, 27,
        30–31, 32, 33
eurozone, 30, 59
ex-officio participants, 20, 43

F

Federal Reserve, 21
finance ministries, 21, 54
France, 5, 11, 15, 16, 33, 37,
        42, 53, 59

G

G8, 4, 11, 23, 24, 25, 28
General Agreement on Tariffs
        and Trade (GATT), 8
Germany, 5, 11, 16, 19, 20,
        32–33, 49, 56
G15, 11

G5, 11
Ghana, 8
global GDP, 10, 25
globalization, 7, 9, 20, 29, 47,
    49, 58
Great Depression, 32
Greece, 31, 33, 59–60
G7, 4, 5, 10, 11, 14, 16, 23, 25,
    28, 31–35, 40, 41
G77, 11, 27
G6, 11
G33, 14, 15
G20
    background of members,
        25–27, 29–40
    criticism of, 58, 60–62
    and global financial crisis,
        23, 40, 43, 51, 53–56
    how it was formed, 14–16
    meetings, 19, 21–23, 31, 36,
        46–50, 51–53, 63
    mission, 20–23
    myths and facts about, 28
    policies and procedures, 42,
        44–46
    structure, 41–42, 63
    summits, 6, 20, 23, 31, 37,
        41, 51, 53–60, 62, 63
G24, 11
G22, 12–14, 15
Guinea, 37

I

India, 6, 8, 27, 35, 36–37, 48
Indonesia, 6, 10, 39

International Bank for
    Reconstruction and
    Development (IBRD),
    19, 43
International Monetary Fund
    (IMF), 12, 15, 19, 20, 25,
    31, 41, 43, 45, 50, 53, 54,
    55, 59, 59, 60, 63
Ireland, 31
Italy, 5, 11, 16, 31, 33, 59, 60

J

Japan, 5, 11, 32

M

Martin, Paul, 14, 16
Mexico, 6, 9, 39, 42, 49, 60

N

Netherlands, 28
9/11 terrorist attacks, 21, 47
nongovernmental organizations, 46
nonmember invitees, 37
North American Free Trade
    Agreement (NAFTA), 9
Norway, 25

O

Organization for Economic
    Co-operation and
    Development, 46

P

Portugal, 31
protests, 58

R

Russia, 4, 6, 11, 25, 27, 35, 37

S

Sarkozy, Nicolas, 59, 60
Saudi Arabia, 6, 39
Sherpas, 44–45
South Africa, 6, 35, 38, 39, 45, 50
South Korea, 6, 10, 39, 42, 53, 56, 58
Spain, 28, 31, 37
Switzerland, 25

T

Thailand, 10
Troika, 42
Turkey, 6, 39

U

United Arab Emirates, 27
United Kingdom, 6, 11, 16, 33, 51
United Nations, 46, 61–62
United States, 6, 9, 11, 18, 21, 27, 32, 33, 35, 36, 39, 56, 58, 63
U.S. Department of the Treasury, 21

W

Wall Street, 4, 51
working groups, 45, 46
World Bank, 19, 20, 41, 43, 45, 50, 55
World Trade Organization (WTO), 8, 22, 46, 62
World War II, 18

ABOUT THE AUTHOR

Corona Brezina has written extensively about economics, including books on stimulus plans, the Great Recession, deflation, imports and exports, the Federal Reserve and monetary policy, and the GDP and GNP. She lives in Chicago, Illinois.

PHOTO CREDITS

Cover, p. 1 (bottom right), cover (headline) istockphoto.com/Lilli Day; p. 5 Pool/Getty Images; pp. 7, 17, 29, 40, 51 Mari Tama/ Getty Images; p. 9 ChinaFotoPress/Getty Images; pp. 12–13, 22, 52 © AP Images; p. 15 Patrick Piel/Gamma-Rapho/Getty Images; pp. 18–19 Hulton Archive/Getty Images; pp. 24–25 Eric Feferberg/AFP/Getty Images; pp. 26 TonyV3112/Shutterstock; p. 30 Lluis Gene/AFP/Getty Images; p. 34 © John Nordell/The Image Works; p. 36 STR/AFP/Getty Images; pp. 38–39 Pete Turner/Riser/Getty Images; p. 42 David Ramos/Getty Images; pp. 44–45 Johannes Eisele/AFP/Getty Images; p. 47 Michael Kappler/AFP/Getty Images; pp. 48–49 William West/AFP/ Getty Images; pp. 56–57 © istockphoto.com/travelinglight; pp. 60–61 Louisa Gouliamaki/AFP/Getty Images; cover (background) and interior graphic elements (financial diagram) © istockphoto.com/Audrey Prokhorov; back cover (background), p. 1 (background) and interior graphic element (world map and financial chart) © istockphoto.com/Turner; © istockphoto.com/ Darja Tokranova (28); © istockphoto.com/articular (p. 63); © istockphoto.com/studiovision (pp. 64, 66, 70–71, 77); multiple interior pages © istockphoto.com/Chen Fu Soh (currency gears).

Designer: Nicole Russo; Photo Researcher: Marty Levick